Actually Useful B2B Selling

by Phil Cohen
Copyright 2013 Phil Cohen, all rights reserved.
ISBN: 1493629913
ISBN-13: 978-1493629916

Contents

Introduction 5

Why most people can't sell 7

What are you selling? 11

Who are you selling to? 17

Making a target list 19

Getting names to call 23

Why are you calling? 25

Scripting the call 27

Hard to get to customers 31

Learning how to listen 33

Digging into problems 37

Record keeping 39

Objections 43

Visits 47

What to take 49

Purpose of the visit 51

Be ready to make the sale 53

Paperwork 55

Referrals 57

Complex sales 61

Quotes, proposals and tenders 65

Delivery 67

Hiring salespeople 69

Online and other promotions 73

Sales metrics 75

Building your business 77

What's next? 79

Introduction

How do you make business-to-business sales from a standing start? No startup business ever started up without sales. This book tells you everything you need to know to take your idea and turn it into a business, or take a small business and turn it into a larger one.

I started my own consulting company in 1985 and learned selling the hard way: I had to either sell or starve. I managed to survive (I still own that company and two others), and later learned professional selling skills from experts; I'm now much better at selling than I was when I started, and this book is kind of from me to my earlier self. This is the book I wish I'd had in 1985.

Phil Cohen, Sydney, 2013

All material copyright Phil Cohen, Sydney, 2013.

Why most people can't sell

All of us have bought stuff from a store. Retail sales works like this: you walk into a shop and look at the goods on display. A sales assistant wanders up to you and asks if you'd like more information, and if you say yes then they tell you about the products in the store.

When you feel you have enough information, you pick up some item and walk it to the register and buy it.

When people start selling business-to-business for the first time, they model their actions on what they already know about selling: retail sales. They think it's about telling the customer about the product and waiting for them to buy.

That's the approach that I took back in 1985 - it didn't work then, and won't work now.

There are a couple of fundamental differences between retail and business-to-business (B2B) sales. The first is that in B2B your customer almost never comes to you. There are very very few businesses where you just sit in your office or factory and wait for the calls to come in. And even if you're lucky enough to have a business like that, you can expand it dramatically by going out and finding more customers.

B2B sales is about going out and approaching customers, about finding them and selling to them. Also, although you'll certainly need to know about your product or service, B2B selling is not about telling your customer about what you have to sell: it's about asking them what they need.

In fact, some expert retail salespeople already do something like this. Let's look at two possible scenarios that might happen to you when you walk into a camera store. You know that you're looking for a camera as a birthday present for your partner, but you're not sure which one to buy.

Scenario 1: You walk into the store and look around. There is a display of brightly-coloured cameras at prices in the range you'd like to pay. You walk over to them and a sales assistant approaches you and asks if you'd like more information about the cameras you're looking at. You say yes, and they start to tell you about the different models, and which one has the most megapixels and the best lens. After a while your eyes glaze over and you say thanks and move away. Maybe you'll buy a camera here, maybe you won't.

Scenario 2: You walk into the store and look around, and stop in front of the brightly-coloured cameras. A sales assistant approaches and asks you if you already have a camera. You say you have, but you're looking to buy one for your partner for their birthday. The sales assistant starts asking questions about your partner's hobbies, and whether they already have a camera. After a while the assistant suggests a compact camera more expensive than the ones you were looking at, but which would be perfect for the person you're buying for. You buy the camera and at the sales assistant's suggestion you also buy a spare battery and some memory cards. They throw in a camera pouch and you're delighted.

Most people, when they start selling B2B, use scenario 1. They call up a potential customer and immediately start unloading all of the product or service information they have in their head. Then they just wait for the customer to say "Okay I'll buy that". But B2B selling just doesn't work that way. It's much more like scenario 2 (although still not exactly the same, as you'll find out in this book).

The other reason people can't sell has to do with their self image, particularly if what they're selling is their own product or service. B2B sales means calling people and trying to sell to them - but not everyone you call will buy. In fact, particularly at the start, you'll end up making the vast majority of the calls to people who either can't or don't want to buy what you have to sell.

If you are bulletproof confident in yourself (or a sociopath) this won't affect you at all. But if you're a normal person, it will.

Imagine that you're fairly confident in your abilities and your product/service at 9 am. You sit down and start calling potential customers. By 11 am you've made 15 phone calls, actually spoken to 10 people, and six of them have told you to call again in a few months. The other four have just told you they're not interested. You take a coffee break.

If you're a normal person you'll be feeling pretty discouraged by this stage. After you finish your coffee you might decide to do some more research, or rearrange the furniture in your office, or go for a walk. Or you might decide to sit down and make 15 more calls. And 15 more after that. And then another 15. At the end of the day you've made 60 calls and you fully expect each of them to be a dud. You wonder why you're doing this at all, and think maybe you should do something else.

That's Monday.

This can go one of two ways: either you start making sales (and I'll show you how to do that in this book) or you give up. Even experienced salespeople 'burn out' and get 'call reluctance' to the point where they just can't make any more calls. They start finding other things to do instead of calling. Or they start drinking, or taking sick days, or just change jobs.

The ability to deal with rejection (and each of those 60 calls will feel like a rejection if you let it) is the other reason most people can't sell. But this book will tell you how to avoid it.

What are you selling?

There was a fashion some years ago for businesses to try to redefine themselves in broader terms. The logic went something like this: if you had owned a horse dealership in the 19th century, you would have been in  danger of being driven out of business by the new motor car industry. But if you'd only thought of yourself as a 'transportation dealership' instead, you would have had the correct attitude to broaden your business base and start selling cars as well as horses.

This is all very well, but not really useful. In practice, you have to know what's coming in order to make the right choice. Instead of a horse dealership, you could have redefined your business as an 'animal dealership' and ended up with a lot of unsaleable kangaroos. It's only the knowledge that the motor car is coming that makes it good business sense to redefine yourself in terms of 'transportation'.

Another trick of the head that businesses like to play with themselves is to think about 'solutions'. So instead of a horse dealership you might consider yourself a dealer in 'transportation solutions'. The idea being that you're not selling cameras, you're selling birthday presents.

Again, that's clever, but not clever enough. You still need to know what problem you're solving before you can provide solutions. So if you're absolutely sure that people only buy cameras as presents, or that there is a big enough market in people looking for presents to support a shop that sells nothing but, then 'present solutions' is okay. Otherwise you're just going to end up with a lot of cheap cameras that work okay as presents but don't suit someone looking for a good camera to spend good money on.

(The idea of being a 'solutions' company came to something of a head when Sydney Water started using the tagline "Delivering solutions". I only hope that their use of the word 'solutions' was deliberately ironic, and that the solutions they deliver are very dilute.)

So how should you define what problem you solve for your customers? The approach that will work best for you is to sell what people are prepared to pay for. Simple, and not that hard to achieve. You just have to find out what problem they need solved. But it's just not good enough to guess - you're going to have to ask them.

This begs the question: "what people"? How can you find out what your target market wants unless you know who they are? The truth of the matter is that what they want to buy and who they are are intertwined questions: you can't really answer one without answering the other. In practice you'll be finding out both answers 'iteratively', meaning that you'll take a guess at your target market and then get an answer for what they want to buy, and then use what they want to buy to refine (and sometimes expand) your definition of your target market. And so on.

So in a sense it doesn't matter where you start, you're going to go round in circles a bit before you find your 'sweet spot' of market and problem to solve.

So let's assume that you have your target market as a starting point and look at what problem you're going to solve. In the next chapter we'll talk about markets and you can refine your initial guess.

Imagine for a moment that you run a travel agency. You've just moved into a new office and it has a great view, but between 4 pm and 5 pm every day the sun shines right in through the big windows and your staff start to fall asleep. There's so much glare that they can't see their computer screens, and they complain about headaches. You realise that there's a bit of a problem, but reckon it will go away during the winter, and it only lasts for an hour a day even during summer. Times are tight in the travel industry, and you're not too worried about staff taking other jobs: there's nowhere else for them to go. And you'd rather spend money on advertising than reducing glare.

This is a typical B2B customer: they have a problem you can solve (if you sell blinds) but it's not top of their priority. They have other things to worry about.

So you can see the difference between this customer and someone who might wander into your blind shop and ask about glare reduction: this travel agency customer has a problem you can solve, but it's not important enough to them to make them go out and seek a solution. They won't be coming to you: you'll have to find them.

Now there are two ways to approach them. You can look at your product as a solution looking for a problem "We have a great range of blinds that can brighten your office, are easy to clean, much cheaper than our competitors, and come in a range of colours." Or as a problem looking for a solution "Glare can reduce your staff's productivity by 50% and can lead to compensation claims. And we can print your company name on your blind so it can be seen from the street, providing ongoing free advertising."

But am I just leading you down the same path as the horse dealership? How do you know that the problem you're trying to solve is really seen as a problem by your target market?

There is only one way to answer that question, and that is to ask them.

Once you have decided what your initial target market is going to be, go and see them and ask them what sorts of problems they have in running their business. There is no substitute for this process, but the good news is that it's pretty easy to do.

Start with people you know who work in your target industry. If you sell to business, talk to people you know who are in business. If you sell to government, talk to people you know who work in government.

Use each conversation to spark the next one "That's been really useful. Can you suggest someone else I could talk to about this as well?"

Resist the temptation to try to make sales during these conversations. You'll find that people will ask to buy from you anyway, and you shouldn't turn them down, but your purpose will be just to gather information, not to sell.

How can you reach people if you don't already know someone in the industry? You'll need to use the tools and techniques you'll learn later in this book to make calls and make visits, and maybe you'll have to read through some more of the book before you can do your research. But before you start selling (or even, as you'll see, before you name your business) come back to here and do the research.

When you contact someone you'd like to talk to, try using this line: "I'm thinking of setting up a <whatever> business and I'd like your advice. Can I buy you a coffee?" Be sure you say you're only thinking of setting up: this will reassure them that you're not going to actually try to sell them something. And a free cup of coffee and a ready ear for advice? Who could resist? Most people love to be asked for advice.

If they say they're too busy, don't forget to ask if there's anyone else they think might be interested in helping. That way, you can call the second person and say "Hi, <first person> suggested you as someone I could go to for advice. I'm thinking of setting up a <whatever> business - can I buy you a coffee and chat about it?"

Once you do get in front of them, remember that you're there to listen, not to talk. Of course, they'll want to know about your business but try to keep that bit short. Have some starter questions ready ("When you buy <whatever>, what do you look for?", "Do you know of other businesses you think I'll be competing with? What are they like?", "What are the main issues you face in doing your job?", "Who makes the decision to buy <whatever> in your business?") but only use them if the conversation flags. You should spend most of your time listening.

And what are you listening for? You're trying to pick up terminology: you'll want to be able to use the same terms and phrases that your customers use when you come to sell to them; this will reassure them that you know their industry. You're also trying to pick up issues that your customers might have, and that you can provide a solution to.

Let me give you a concrete example. You're going to set up a water cooler rental business, and you know that most of the people who rent water coolers are business with at least 10 employees. Your second cousin works as an accountant in an insurance company, so you call her.

You ask if you can buy her a coffee and ask for some advice. You talk to her and notice that when she talks about water coolers she refers to them as one of a number of 'staff amenities': this is a phrase you write down, because when you call potential customers in future you'll want to use it. She tells you that the office manager usually decides what to spend on staff amenities, and that they have an annual budget to spend. And so on. All of this is very valuable information, because it will let you shape your business and make your first sales.

In this example, you'll be calling potential clients and asking to speak to the office manager. You'll then be able to ask them if they're responsible for the office's staff amenities budget. How much more effective is that, instead of calling a potential client and asking "who looks after the water coolers"? You may even want to change your business focus from "Watercoolers Inc" to "Staff Amenities R Us" and start renting refrigerators as well as water coolers.

Of course, you shouldn't make these changes just on one conversation with your second cousin: you'll need to keep talking to people until you see a pattern that you're sure of.

One key skill you'll need in this process, and in the rest of your sales career, is the ability to listen. I'll cover that later in this book.

Who are you selling to?

Once you've done your initial research (by talking to a bunch of people in target customers) you'll probably have changed your ideas about what you want to sell, or at the very least what you want to call it.

Now's the time to go back round the loop and ask again who you want to sell to. For example, if you started off deciding to sell blinds to offices, but found that people weren't interested in buying blinds, they were interested in stopping glare, then you might have decided to broaden your product line to include other glare-stopping products like glass coatings. You might have changed your business focus from "Office Blinds Inc" to "Glarestoppers".

Then you'd want to go back and revisit your target market decision. If you are now about stopping glare, rather than selling blinds, maybe you could broaden your target market to factories as well as offices? Factories might not be a suitable place for blinds, but they may buy glass coating instead.

So start thinking about who you know that works in a factory, and take them out for coffee.

This is what's called an 'iterative' process, meaning that you'll bounce back and forth between product/service definition and target market definition, and it might take you a while to settle on exactly what problem you're going to solve and who you're going to solve it for.

It's worth doing, though, because if you don't do it before you start your business, you're going to end up doing it after your business is already up and running. And that's much much harder.

It's harder for a number of reasons: the main one being your own enthusiasm. You've got yourself excited about selling blinds to offices, and have spent time working out your new company's name, checked that no-one else is using it, and registered it. Perhaps even got fliers and business cards printed and started making sales calls and told all of your friends and family that you're in the blinds business. Imagine how hard it is to then change your mind and be in the glare reduction business, throw away that company name that you've fantasised about turning into a multinational, chuck out your newly-minted business cards and promotional material and tell all of your friends that you got it wrong first time round. No, it'll be too tempting to just keep banging your head against the original market and the original product/service set that you came up with until the whole thing falls in a heap.

So do your homework first. Then commit.

Making a target list

Once you've (finally) decided who you're selling to and what problem you're solving, you can start building a list of target organisations.

A good way to start is to ask yourself "who is my ideal customer?" This is a question that many organisations use to refine their ideas about markets. It's a useful one because the alternative question "who might we sell to?" is just too broad and will result in an ill-defined and vague set of parameters. You'll need something a lot more focussed, particularly at the start.

So sit down and write out what your ideal customer organisation looks like. What industry are they in? How many staff do they have? What products/services do they currently use in your space (if you're selling blinds, do they already have them, or do they have none)? What city are they based in? What's their annual turnover? You can only have one ideal customer, so resist the temptation to make your definition too broad. If you really have more than one ideal customer, pick the one that's *most* ideal.

Now you'll have a definition for your target list, and you can use it to build an initial list. At this stage it will be a list of organisations, rather than a list of individuals within those organisations.

How you do this will depend on who you're trying to sell to. If your ideal customer is a government department, your list will be a small one, and you'll be able to build it by going onto the government's web site and getting a list of departments. Simple.

If your target is in a particular industry, there are industry association web sites that may provide member lists. Or some magazines will run 'top 100' stories for particular industries, so you can find targets there.

Just doing a web search for the industry that you're looking for can work, too.

If you've defined your target by location, you can use online maps to look for businesses within an area. Or you can just walk the location yourself and make a list. (If you're selling glare reduction you might visit some office blocks that get a lot of sun, and make a list of the companies on the sunny side of the block, for example).

Remember at this stage you're not trying to narrow your targets; resist the temptation to say "Oh I'm sure a big company like that will have this covered, I won't bother putting them on the list". If they match your ideal client, they go on the list.

If you need to, there are companies like Dun and Bradstreet who will sell you access to their database of companies, and you can search for particular industries, locations and even company size. But you should avoid that if you can do the same thing for free.

If you're having trouble building a list like this, maybe your ideal customer is too vague. Go back and refine it.

How many organisations should be on your target list? That will depend on how much you can make out of them. If you've decided that you're going to sell to government departments and there are only 20 of them, then you're never going to get more than 20 customers. If you look at that list and say "well, even if I sell to all 20 I still won't have a viable business" then maybe that's trying to tell you something: you don't have a viable business idea, so go back and rethink it.

If you look at the list of 20 departments and say "if I only sell to five of them I'll be able to retire", then you're good to go.

Similarly if you are only going to make $1000 from each sale, you'll need a bigger target list than if you're going to make $10,000 from each of them. Decide on your list size depending on how many customers you need to get going. And if there aren't enough of those kinds of companies to make the size of list you need, rethink what you're doing.

Getting names to call

Now you have your initial target list, you can start to collect names of people to talk to within those organisations. The person you ideally want to talk to is the one who can, on their own initiative, make the decision to buy what you have to sell.

Sometimes that person doesn't exist, because of the nature of what you sell. Large, complex sales often involve selling to more than one person in the target organisation, but we'll leave that aside for now and come back to it later.

Go back to your 'ideal customer' and ask yourself, from what you know about those types of organisation, who is likely to be able to make the decision you need. The more you know about your target market, the better. A job title is ideal. If you need help with working out what job title your target has, buy some more coffees and do some more research.

Remember that you'll need to find someone who can make the purchase decision on their own (if they exist) but don't go too high. Yes, the MD can probably decide which water cooler to rent, but they're unlikely to actually make that decision if the target organisation is of any size at all.

Similarly, don't go too low. If you need to talk to the Office Manager, don't settle for targeting the Receptionist just because they're easier to get to.

It would be tempting to start calling the target firms and getting the names of the people you need to sell to, but don't do that yet. The easiest way to find out the name of, say, the Office Manager is to call the switchboard at the company and ask them for the name. But half of the time they won't just tell you the name, they'll put you through. You're not ready for that yet, so just hold on to the job title and the target list for now.

Why are you calling?

Now you need to think about the process that your customer is going to go through to buy your product or service. Take a sheet of paper and write down the likely steps.

Will they want to see you in their office, or will they just buy over the phone?

If they want to see you, will they want you to talk to someone else as well (procurement, maybe, or the IT department if you're selling software)?

Is what you're selling big enough that they'll have to put out a tender or get three quotes before they're allowed to buy it? (This is particularly relevant to government customers).

Write down the steps that they'll need to go through in order to buy what you have to sell. This is called their 'buying process'. What you do next depends on what this process looks like, so check with one of your contacts that you've got it right. Or just start making calls and see what happens: if you're wrong it won't take you long to find out.

There are very few products or services that you can sell over the phone to an organisation without further contact. The second step in their buying process (after your initial phone call) might be for you to send them some paperwork in the mail, or send them an email, or go see them. Before you make your first call, you should have an idea of what that second step might be - and **getting that second step to happen is the purpose, the sole purpose, of your call**.

So without all this preparation your call may have gone something like this:

"Hi, are you the person who orders office blinds? Well we have a great range of blinds that come in all sorts of colours and ... oh, they hung up."

Now you can make this call:

"Hi, is that the Office Manager? 'd like to come and show you how you can improve staff productivity by cutting down on glare."

Notice how almost the first thing out of your mouth is the second step in their buying process: a visit. You're not going to try to sell them over the phone, because you know that just doesn't happen. You're also using some of the terminology that you've picked up from your research ('office manager', 'improve staff productivity') and you're addressing the main problem that you've identified in your research (reducing glare). In fact, you haven't even needed to mention blinds, even though that's what you're trying to sell.

The ideal initial call gets you to step 2 in the buying process, and that's all. Sure, if they say they'd like to buy some blinds over the phone you're not going to say no, but that's not the purpose of the call.

Being certain about your call's purpose means you can make more calls in a day, and means that you can focus on the outcome you want. It makes you sound authoritative, and easy to deal with.

Scripting the call

Now that you know who you're going to call and why you're calling, you can start writing a *script* for your call. If you haven't done any 'cold calling' before this will be very valuable. Of course,  like any script you'll only need it for the first few calls. In fact, you should make sure that you don't become dependent on the script, otherwise you'll sound like a robot.

How do you create a script that works? There are some common elements.

First you have to identify that you've got the right person and the right organisation. "Hi, is that the office manager for <customer name>?"

Check that they're not in the middle of something: "Is this a good time to talk?"

Then you have to tell them what's in it for them "I'd like to come and show you how to improve staff productivity ..."

Wait a beat to let them absorb what you just said, and (possibly) say you've got the wrong person, or the wrong company (it happens) or that they're just not interested.

If they just say yes, or "uhuh?" then you're nearly done, do a 'trial close' for the call "How does Tuesday at 2 pm sound?"

If they say yes, then the call worked and you're finished. Just say "Okay I'll see you then. Goodbye." and hang up.

The script is going to depend very much on what you expect the buying process to look like. If you think they'll buy over the phone, you won't be asking them for a visit.

And the content of the script will also depend on how you normally speak ... after all, you're going to be the one using it.

Finally, it will change as you use it and make improvements.

Once you've got your script done, try it out on a friend. Have them pretend to be a customer and say the things they think the customer might say. Make a game of it, and have them give you feedback on how you did.

You'll want to change the script a few times before you're ready to 'road test' it.

Then you can start using it. You've got your customer list so you can start collecting actual names now. Call the switch at each company and ask for the name of the person whose job title you need.

"Hi, this is <your name> from <your company>. Could you tell me the name of your <job title>, please?" Simple as that.

If they put you through to the person you're trying to find the name of (instead of just giving you the name), you will have your script to fall back on. If they just give you the name, just write it down and move onto the next customer on your list.

If you can find names from job titles without making phone calls, all the better. Sometimes you'll come across a fantastic list of potential customers with all of their names and phone numbers already researched, and this is golden. An excellent source is any seminar that those kinds of people (office managers, or whatever) will attend. Seminar organisations will always keep a list of attendees and their contact details, and sometimes you can get hold of them by just attending and asking for the list afterwards. Sometimes you'll have to buy it.

Hard to get to customers

If the person you're trying to reach is senior in the organisation, you'll probably come across a 'gatekeeper'. This is the person on the switchboard, or a personal assistant, who will give you the third degree before they'll even tell you the name of the person you're after, far less connect you.

Be prepared to sell to these people as well - although they're not going to buy your product, they will still need to be convinced that you're worth their boss' time to talk to.

The conversation might go like this:

"Hi, I'm John Smith from Glarestoppers. Could you tell me the name of your Office Manager, please?"

"Will he know who you are?"

"No, he won't, but I'll be talking to him about office glare and the fact that your building faces right into the setting sun. We help companies like yours to improve productivity and I'm sure he'll want to talk to me about that."

"Well, okay, I'll put you through."

For more senior people still the closest you'll get on a first call will be a personal assistant ("PA"). These are not just secretaries, they're really more like deputies. In fact, if you're trying to reach a CFO or a CEO you should really just target their PA, like this:

"Hi, this is John Smith from Bankchoosers. I understand that Karen Smith is your CFO ... but could you tell me the name of her PA?"

Then you make the call to the PA, and sell them on your idea. They will often ask you to send an email, so that they can discuss your offer with their boss before allowing you to make contact. Again, you'll be selling to the PA in the same way you'll be selling to the boss - explain to them how you'll be solving one of their boss's problems and you'll get through.

Sometimes you just hit a brick wall: "Well, if he doesn't know who you are, then I can't put you through." Try to go around them - if you can't get to the CFO maybe try someone else in the Finance department, who can then introduce you to the CFO without going through their PA.

Learning how to listen

Remember the camera store example? One of the hardest things to do in selling is to shut up and listen. Camera salespeople sell more when they ask questions and then listen to what customers tell them, rather than 'spray and pray' - just bombarding the customer with specifications and features and hoping that they'll buy.

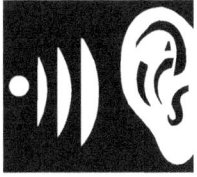

Listening is like any other skill: you get better with practice. Here's an exercise you should do with a friend (or even better, your partner) to build the ability to listen.

Set a timer and ask them to talk about their day for a full five minutes. During that time you have to listen to them *without saying a word*. At the end of five minutes, you have to talk for *one full minute* without stopping, about what you just heard.

This is much much harder than it sounds. If you interrupt during the five minutes, you fail. If you zone out during the five minutes, you won't be able to talk for a full minute when it's your turn.

Don't just do it once; keep doing it until you feel comfortable just listening. Then (and this is the really hard part) remember to do that listening when you're nervously making your first sales calls!

Just to make it more interesting, swap roles so that you're talking and the other person is listening. (Hey, it might even save your relationship too.)

An advanced form of listening is called 'active listening', where you are allowed to make the odd noise or comment, but not interrupt. For example, you might say "Really?" or "Of course" where appropriate, or reflect what the person just told me "So you're saying that the glare is really causing you problems?". Active listening is what we mostly do without thinking when we're listening ... but of course the other thing we do mostly when we're not thinking is to interrupt and then start talking ourselves.

While using active listening, you should be careful about the kind of comment you make. For example, don't disagree with what you've been told.

Try to ask 'open' questions (if you have to ask questions at all): an open question is one with a long answer. For example, "How many staff do you have?" is not an open question because it has a short answer. But "What do your staff think about glare?" has a long answer.

There's a lot of reading you can do about listening technique. You'll find that changing the way you listen will take days or even weeks. One of the best ways to improve is to come out of each phone conversation (or each face to face sales meeting) and just ask yourself silently if you did a good or a bad job of listening that time.

Having someone listen to you, particularly if they sound interested and you're talking about something you feel strongly about, is for most people a very satisfying experience. They'll come out of that conversation feeling that the person they just spoke to (ie you) was empathetic, intelligent, and had their best interest at heart. You'll also find out a lot more about them (and how your business can help them) than if you just launches into a long lecture about what you do and how good it is.

Digging into problems

There are a number of sales methodologies that are based on asking specific kinds of questions: questions that expose problems that the customer hadn't really thought deeply about until you asked.

For example, you might ask "So there's a lot of glare around four o'clock each day. What effect does that have on your staff?" And then you might follow up with "So if they're sleepy and unmotivated, what effect does that have on their productivity?" And perhaps "Well if they're losing almost an hour a day, what effect is that going to have on your bottom line? It's like paying them almost 10% extra."

By asking questions like this you can (with practice) dig into your potential customer's problems, expose them to the light, and make them think about how bad they are and what kinds of long-term effects they might have. As you do this, you'll find the prospect will get more and more concerned about the problems you're discussing. Then at the end you can offer a solution and their mood will brighten.

If you do this right (and don't expect it to work perfectly the first dozen times you try, or reliably even after that) then the mood of the conversation will start 'up' as you introduce yourself and start listening, but will drop into a hole as you uncover the problems, then come 'up' again at the other end as you offer a solution.

This general approach is used in a variety of contexts (some therapies, some interrogation techniques) and it's very powerful.

When you start practicing these techniques you'll notice that good salespeople who try to sell you things will try to use similar techniques on you: but you won't mind. After all, the purpose is just to make you aware of problems you might not have thought about, and offer a solution.

You'll also become super-sensitive to bad salespeople who just 'spray and pray'.

Record keeping

I don't know about you, but I can't remember every detail of every conversation that I've had over the past six months. If you can do that, then you can skip this section of the book. Otherwise, read on.

Your aim in the second sales conversation that you have with someone should be to build on the first conversation, rather than repeat it. That means that all of the good stuff that you got from all of that active listening the first time round needs to be in your head while you're having conversation number two.

Assuming that each conversation might be days or weeks apart, that means writing stuff down. For every one of my sales conversations, whether by phone or face to face, I write a couple of paragraphs about the key things that were discussed, actions agreed and other details.

Here's a real extract from one of my notes (names changed to protect the guilty): "Called John and asked whether he'd read the proposal. He said he had, but that he'd have to discuss it with his boss (Sarah) before they went ahead. He did say he thought the cost might be "prohibitive" so I asked if he had a budget in mind, but he said no. I asked who else in the company might be interested in what we do and he said he'd think about it. Suggested I call him next month after their steering group meeting on the 15th. I asked if he would be comfortable talking to Sarah directly but he got very nervous at that so I let it go."

The time to start taking detailed notes of your conversations is *now*. The sooner you start, the easier it will be for you to get into the habit, and the more value you notes will be to you in the future.

As your business grows, they'll be even more use, because you can share the sales workload with someone else.

Of course, as well as notes about your conversations you'll want to record details of the names and addresses, phone numbers and email addresses of your potential customers. This is even more valuable, because you can start doing mass mailings and using other labour-saving sales approaches.

The logical place to keep both kinds of information (names and details, and notes) is in a Customer Relations Management (CRM) system. There are a large number of these available and they range from free to very expensive. My advice would be to start with a free one; you can always move the data to a bigger more extensive one later. The most important part of any business software system is the information in it (not the software itself) so I'd focus on actually recording information, rather than worrying about how to store and retrieve it at this stage.

My first CRM system was one sheet of plain paper for each potential client company. I wrote all of the contact details on the top half of the page, and wrote the notes on the bottom half. I kept the pieces of paper in alphabetical order of company name so I could find them. It worked really well and it cost me nothing.

Objections

One of the things that you'll find people do when you try to sell them is to make objections. These can range from the vague "we're not ready to make a decision yet" to the very specific "your software doesn't run on our brand of computers".

There are two things you need to know about objections: 1) they're only real sometimes, and 2) they're valuable to you.

Why would someone make an objection that wasn't real? I bet you do it all the time: when a charity worker approaches you looking for a donation you don't say what you really think ("I don't like being approached in the street by strangers asking for money."), you give a false objection ("I gave at the office").

People make false objections when they don't want to tell you the real one, either because they're embarrassed, or they can't be bothered. In B2B sales the most common false objection you'll hear is "send me a written proposal and I'll think about it." That usually means "I'm not going to buy, but I don't want to tell you the reason, and I don't want to hurt your feelings because you sound like a nice person".

Of course you have to be careful: what if they really do want a written proposal and they really will think about it? That's always possible and after a while you'll be able to tell the difference, but it's best to start with the assumption that it's just a false objection otherwise you'll spend a lot of time writing pointless proposals (I know I did).

Another false objection is "we don't have the budget for that right now". There isn't a business on the planet that couldn't find money for something that they think is worthwhile, whether it's in this year's budget or not. If the person you're talking about can't make that happen, then you're talking to the wrong person.

Yet another possibly false objection: "we've decided to go with another supplier". Again, sometimes that's just the truth: but you should always ask who they've gone with, and why.

The kind of information you get from *real* objections is very valuable. After all, if you know why they *didn't* buy, you can hopefully do something about it for next time. One of the things you can do is to pre-empt the objection, or at least provide a 'counter' to it.

Let's say that a lot of people say your glare-proofing will need approval from the building owner before you can install it. You can pre-empt that objection by working into your initial conversation the fact that as part of your service you're happy to do the work to get that approval (maybe you can even charge extra for it?).

You can simply collect objections as you come across them, and then decide what the counter is for each one for next time, or you can brainstorm a bunch of objections and work out their counters before you start. For very large sales (for example, multi-million-dollar sales presentations) people will do just this: they'll work out all of the questions that they *don't* want to be asked, and then work out the answer to each one before they're asked.

Visits

All of the information I've given you up to this point has been applicable to conversations that you have with your customers by phone, or face to face. Of course, there are  some things that are unique to a face to face visit.

You should always aim to dress slightly *more* formally than your customer. If they're a dot com and always dress in T-shirts, you should be smart casual. If they dress smart casual, you should dress in business standard. If they dress business standard, you should dress in business formal.

Remember that the level of formality that you can expect in a client will depend on a number of things, but mainly on their industry. Lawyers will be somewhere at the top, and software developers somewhere near the bottom.

Always turn up 5-10 minutes before the meeting time. It will take a few minutes for you to sign in at reception and for them to come and find you. Don't turn up 20 minutes early (they'll get confused and think they (or you) have got the time wrong) and *never* turn up late.

Personally, I plan my journey to get to a meeting a full 25 minutes early, then go for a walk or read my notes outside until 10 minutes before time. Although it sounds like I've wasted 15 minutes the fact that I arrive relaxed and on time more than makes up for it. And if the traffic's bad I even have an extra 15 minutes in hand in case I need it. Works for me.

Remember that when you're in the meeting you're doing the active listening thing. From the moment you arrive. Until the moment you leave.

The best sales meeting I ever had was with a university administrator; he came in and we swapped cards, and then he talked continuously for 40 minutes (I literally listened the whole time) and then he ended the conversation with "Well, I think we'll go ahead. What you're offering is just what we need." Do you think that I had a problem with that?

There's an old sales joke that goes "Wait, you can't buy yet, you haven't heard my pitch". People will buy based on what *they* say, not on what *you* say.

What to take

Most B2B salespeople will carry 'collateral' with them. This is generally printed material that describes the products and services that you sell,  or some aspect of your organisation. Often the printing is glossy, and there's an expectation that this material will help make the sale.

I used to make sales visits complete with a mini flipchart with A4 slides that I could show the customer, and a glossily printed folder which held loose leaf brochures on what I hoped to sell. These days would use an iPad or similar, if I still took materials with me on sales visits. But I no longer take any materials.

What I found was that having materials with me tempted me to start talking, and that every word I said took me further from the sale. During that visit that I described earlier (where the university administrator talked for 40 minutes) the only piece of collateral I gave him was my business card.

There is a place for collateral (and for its online equivalent, the web site) in B2B selling but it's useful mainly to convince the customer that your organisation is large enough to be safe to deal with. Collateral is no substitute for listening. The purpose of the collateral is to say "we're a big enough organisation to be able to afford glossy printing".

Marketing people love to generate collateral, newsletters, 'with compliments' slips and other material that 'builds the brand'. But what I've found is that most of that gets in the way, and other than convincing your potential customer that you're large enough to waste money on that kind of thing, won't actually help make any sales.

Purpose of the visit

In exactly the same way that you defined the purpose of your first phone call to this customer, you should define why you're making the visit: what is it you want to get out of this?

Don't make the mistake of thinking that just being in the same room as a customer will somehow eventually lead to a sale. That just isn't so. You'll need to know what it is you're trying to achieve, otherwise it's just a social visit, and they're worth very little in commercial terms.

Make sure that you write down on your contact sheet what you'd like to achieve out of this meeting. After all, each meeting - including setting it up, travel, making notes afterwards - will cost you several hours, so it had better be worth your while.

Some things you might want to achieve are: getting a signature on an order (ideal), asking questions to expose more issues (but only if you can't for some reason do that in a phone call), demonstrating a product (unless you can do that over the web), convincing the client to do something (again, only if you can't do it over the phone) such as introducing you to a more senior person.

Be sparing with your visits. When a customer says to you on the phone "I think it would be a good idea for us to meet" then you don't have to say yes right away - or at all. Some people love to fill their day with supplier visits because it makes them feel important. I've had clients where I've made three or four visits before realising that I'm just there to give them something to do. Don't make that mistake (I don't, any more).

It's much harder to script a face to face visit than a phone call ... for one thing, when you're on the phone they can't see that you're referring to a script! But before you make the visit make sure that you've thought about what information you need to get from the customer, and what you need to say to them.

Be ready to make the sale

One of the hardest things to do when you're starting out is to 'close the deal'. This is the term that salespeople use to describe the process of asking the customer to buy. Sometimes salespeople will be great at  getting rapport with a customer, fantastic at uncovering their issues and addressing them, and marvellous at describing how we can help. But they sell *nothing*, because they can't bring themselves to 'close'.

Closing just means asking something like "Well, I'll draw up a contract and send it over to you for signature." Or more simply "So, you'll buy <product>; when would you like to take delivery?"

The hard part about closing is that it opens you to failure. If you're having a nice discussion with the customer, you haven't (yet) failed to sell to them. The moment you try to close and they say 'no', you've failed to sell.

So salespeople will go on multiple visits and just keep talking because the last time they tried to close (perhaps with another customer) they got rejected. So they subconsciously avoid that happening again by not closing.

But there are two errors with that approach. The first is that if you don't close, you won't sell (and that's kind of the point, isn't it?). The other is that if you try to close and they say no, it's not over.

In fact, there is a lot in the sale training literature about 'trial closes'; conversational gambits like saying "Well, what else do I need to tell you before you're ready to buy?" Or just asking them to buy, and if they say no, keeping going so that you can ask them again later.

If you play chess, think of a trial close as a 'check'. It's not the end of the game, it just means that you've come close to winning. If you fail this time, keep trying until you get checkmate.

One very valuable purpose for a 'trial close' is to uncover objections. Simply: if they say 'no', you can ask 'why not?'.

And don't be surprised when they say 'yes'! Make sure that you know what to do to make the sale happen - have a contact or order with you ready for them to sign. And try not to look surprised. Definitely don't say "are you sure?"!

Paperwork

Since it's your company you'll want to make sure that every sale is properly documented. You'll want to get a signature on something to prove that your customer has actually bought a product  or service from you ... otherwise you may find that there is some dispute when you try to get paid.

Most small businesses that fail (and many of them do) do so because they have problems getting paid by (usually larger) customers. Often this is the direct result of not getting sufficient paperwork to convince a large organisation to pay, even after delivery. After all, large organisations don't get large by giving money away: they tend to have very restrictive rules on who they give money to, often involving legal proof of purchase.

Better still, insist on payment in advance.

For a more complete treatment of this subject, plus a bunch of other useful stuff, see one of my other books "Actually Useful Accounting".

Referrals

One of the most valuable outcomes from a successful sale is one or more 'referrals'. A referral is simply where a customer (or even a potential customer) gives you the name of another person or organisation that might also be interested in what you have to sell.

Depending on what you're selling, referrals can be within the same organisation ("Go and see Joe in Accounting, he might be interested") in another organisation ("Our supplier might also be interested in this") or even through a personal connection ("My cousin works in a similar business …").

Satisfied customers will often recommend you to others, and may even contact you with referrals. But don't wait for that: *ask* for them.

The best time to ask is when the customer is at their most satisfied with your service or product: perhaps just after delivery. Don't be afraid to ask them to suggest other people for you to talk to. The worst that can happen is they say no.

When taking up referrals, use your connection with the referrer to its maximum effect: "I've just been speaking to Joe Smith and he said I should call you to talk about our product.". Even if Joe had only mentioned the name of the person in passing, you can still make it sound (without actually bending the truth) as if Joe was anxious for you to talk to the new customer.

If you're just starting out in business, and you're lucky enough to make a sale to a large enterprise, then 'leverage' that sale in your calls to other potential customers. Call their competitors and say "we're doing a lot of work with <client> and I think it might be something you're interested in".

If you have a particularly satisfied customer, you can ask them for a written reference (also called a 'testimonial'). These are golden, because you can include them in proposals to other customers. Often people will ask to speak to a number of previous customers ("referees") but a printed reference is even better: it means that you know what's been said about you, for one thing.

You'll often be able to get a written reference like this:

Customer: "Well, I'd just like to say that the blinds have been installed and they make a big difference."

You: "So do you think they'll pay for themselves?"

"Oh, absolutely."

"Well, could I ask you to put that in writing so I can show other people?"

"Er. Sure, I guess so."

"In fact, to save you time I could draft something and send it to you. Of course you're welcome to change it any way you see fit, but then all you'd have to do would be to print it on letterhead and send it back to me. I don't want to put you to any trouble, after all."

This way you can avoid the situation where they never actually get around to writing you a reference (which is likely) and you can also control to some extent what goes in the letter. Make sure that you mention the particular *problem* that you were solving (ie don't just say what kind of blinds you installed) - remember that your next customer is likely to have the same problem and will be impressed by your ability to solve it.

Complex sales

Of course, not all sales decisions are made by a single person. Often you'll be involved in 'complex sales', which are sales where the decision-making process is spread over several people within your customer organisation.

This means more work, but hopefully it also means more revenue because complex sales tend to be bigger.

One of the first things you'll have to do for a complex sale is to find out who all of the people are that you'll have to talk to. Sometimes it can be useful for you to categorise them by the level of influence they are going to have over the decision.

For example, there might be some people who can make the decision *not* to proceed all on their own (if they could make the decision *to* proceed, maybe it wouldn't be a complex sale - all you'd have to do would be to convince them).

Then there are people whose opinion will be important to the sale, but who on their own won't actually be making the decision.

Finally there will be people who will have some influence on the sale, but not much.

For really complex sales, you might have people in one or more of these categories who don't even work for your client company: union delegates, external auditors, consulting firms.

Various sales methodologies have different names for these classes of people: decision makers, influencers, etc, but regardless of what you call them you need to remember that for a complex sale there's going to be more than one person making the decision.

It's a great temptation to focus on the person in a client company who is easiest for you to talk to. In a complex sale, this is a mistake. Let me give you a story to illustrate this.

SellerCo is a software company and sells a piece of software that puts a warning on each user's screen once an hour to tell them to get up and stretch. This has been found to reduce the incidence of work-related injury (particularly carpal tunnel syndrome) and therefore reduce the risk that the client company will be sued for not looking after their employees.

The decision to buy the SellerCo software is normally made by a variety of people within each customer: the Occupational Health and Safety (OHS) Manager is normally very interested, as is any Director of the company (they're the ones who will be sued, after all). The IT Department needs to get involved, and of course Finance needs to know about costs, contracts, etc.

James from SellerCo is an ex OHS Manager and gets on well with the BuyerCo OHS Manager; turns out they know each other from the OHS Association committee from a few years back. James visits the BuyerCo OHS Manager (Janet) and tells her about the SellerCo software -

she's very enthusiastic and says she'll ask for the funding.

James leaves her to it, happy that he's got someone in BuyerCo who will make the sale for him.

Janet calls him a couple of weeks later, and apologises: she can't get budget for the software, even though she thinks it's obviously worth the money. Turns out that the IT Department has been angling for an upgrade to all of the computer operating systems, and the SellerCo software would make this necessary - the current version of SellerCo won't run on the operating system they're currently running. The CFO knocked back the software upgrade on the basis that it would be too expensive. Instead they've decided to put up some posters warning people to get up and stretch once an hour.

James lost the sale. What would have happened if he'd asked Janet who else would be involved in the decision, and then going and talked to them? He might have found out about the operating system issue and offered an older version of the SellerCo software that would work with their existing operating system.

He might have met with the CFO and pointed out that although putting up posters might reduce the company's liability in the event of a problem, the SellerCo software has also been shown to improve productivity (people are generally more motivated when they get up once an hour). If John had realised that this was a complex sale (ie that the decision wasn't Janet's alone) he might have made the sale instead of having to walk away. Because, having put the IT Department and the Finance Department in a position where they've already knocked back the software, he's unlikely to be able to change their minds now no matter what.

What caused John to make this mistake? He focussed on his relationship with Janet, instead of exploring the other decision-makers and influencers in the target organisation.

There are many tools and techniques that you can use to manage complex sales, such as software to allow you to 'map' the influences in the target organisation. But in my experience they all suffer from the same problem: people tend not to use them, because they take time and effort to master and to work with.

That's not to say they're not valuable: they are. But they're *very* hard to implement. If you think that you have the discipline to use one of these tools, go ahead. Otherwise, just make a list of people you need to deal with in each complex sale.

Quotes, proposals and tenders

Remember what I said earlier about a customer asking you for a proposal, and how that was often a 'false objection'? I said that was only true some of the time, and that you had to use your own judgement about  when that was a false objection, and when they actually wanted a proposal so they could buy.

Very little business these days happens 'on a handshake'. You'll always have some paperwork to show that you've made the sale (a purchase order, or a signed contract) and before you get to that you'll often be asked to send a written proposal.

There are whole books on how to write an effective proposal (I'd highly recommend the "Shipley Proposal Guide", although I have to admit a commercial bias here) so I'm not going to go into much detail here. However, I will give you some pointers.

There are no definitions for the difference between a 'quote' and a 'proposal' (I'll come to 'tender' later). But generally a 'quote' has more focus on pricing and a 'proposal' has more focus on selling. And there is no accepted definition of what goes in a quote or a proposal.

Given that there's a bit of confusion about what these terms mean, your only option is to ask your customer exactly what they want. Do they want pricing? Will they be showing the document to other people in the organisation (and if so, should you make contact and talk to them first?). What are their expectations on pricing, and what do they think the main benefits are of what you're trying to sell? Do they need a draft contract? Referees?

The basis on which I operate is this: there should be no surprises for the customer in any proposal or quote. You probably won't be in the room when they open it, so if there's anything you need to do to sell them or prepare them for, you'll have to do it while you're talking to them, and *before* you send the proposal.

In any quote or proposal, make sure you cover off any and all legal requirements (payment terms, warranties (or lack of), how long the pricing is valid, etc). Again, this book is not the place for a detailed discussion of the legalities of sales - my only recommendation would be to try to get hold of a number of proposals for similar products/services and include all of the legal cutouts and defences that you find in *all* of them. And then hire a lawyer to check your standard terms and conditions.

Tenders are different. They come about when your customer initiates a formal process to ask you and some other suppliers to provide competing proposals, usually to a closely-defined format set by the customer. Again, there are books written on this subject (including the Shipley Proposal Guide) and I'd recommend you take a look at at least one of them if you have to respond to tenders.

Another word of advice on tenders: if you can possibly avoid them, try to do so. They're a lot of work.

Delivery

The easiest way to generate new sales leads is to do a good job of delivering. By 'delivering' I don't just mean when the truck turns up at the customer premises, I mean everything you do as a company after the sale is made.

As a minimum, if you make a sale, your job doesn't finish there. Make sure that you visit the customer once they've taken delivery and ask them how it's going. If you've promised particular results over a long period, make sure to call after a while and ask if the results have been forthcoming.

You'd (pretty obviously) do this if there's a chance that you'll sell them something more on top of the original sale. But even if that's not the case it's well worth the visit because you as a salesperson can then bring back improvements to your delivery that will create more sales in the future.

Where you have a happy client, they will generate more clients. In fact, there's a measure widely used in marketing called a Net Promoter Score which (without going into detail) measures whether your customers will recommend you to others. Some very large organisations have spent a lot of money measuring (and figuring out how to improve) this. Anything that you can do as a salesperson to improve the impression that your customers have of your organisation will return dividends to you.

Hiring salespeople

At some point you'll hopefully generate enough sales to hire some staff. And some of them will be salespeople.

Salespeople are created by taking a set of *aptitudes* and adding a set of *skills*. The aptitudes that a salesperson needs are largely built around their own feelings of self-worth and are therefore pretty much 'dyed in the wool': without heavy-duty counselling you can't really change what someone thinks about themselves, so you pretty much have to take what you get in each individual.

Depending on what's in there, you might end up with a salesperson who can't pick up the phone to make a sales call because they believe deep down that the person at the other end doesn't want to talk to them. Or you might end up with someone who insults prospective customers because they have so much to prove to themselves about what they're worth to society. Or you might end up with a salesperson who is so comfortable with their own worth that they can call people and not insult them, and thereby actually make sales.

Another essential element of their aptitude is the intelligence to understand what they're selling, at least to the level that the customer understands it. They don't have to understand it well enough to deliver it, just well enough to understand why someone would buy it.

Once you have someone with the right aptitude, you need to add sales skills like how to:

- listen for what your customer actually wants to buy
- ask questions to make them want to buy
- keep records of who you've talked to and what they said
- make phone calls that result in meetings
- make meetings that result in proposals
- make proposals that result in sales

As with any job, the best predictor of future performance is past performance. Before you hire *anyone* you should look at a detailed resume (CV if that's what you prefer to call it) and look at whether:

- they have provided enough information so that you can see what they've done every year since they left school - if there are gaps they may have been in jail or unemployed (not that you wouldn't hire someone who'd been in jail, just that you'd hope they would be honest enough to tell you about it)
- they have actually done sales before, of the kind that you're going to ask them to do (working in a shoe shop may not qualify!)
- they look as if they stay with each employer for longer than a year (it sometimes takes months for an employer to spot a dud, and so someone who has spent 9 months in each of their last four jobs is suspect)

You should also ask them what their sales target was for their last three jobs, and get the names of a referee for each job that you can call to check them out.

Referees should be people they reported directly to (ie not just someone they befriended who worked in the next cubicle). Call them and ask the following key questions:

- did they actually work in that job title for the period it says on their resume?
- what was their sales target and did they meet it?
- did they report directly to you?
- how did they get on with the rest of their team?
- why did they leave?
- if we hire them, what's your advice about how to get the best out of them?
- what were their strengths?
- what was their single biggest weakness?
- and don't forget to ask ... "do you need any <your product/service>, because it's what we do"

I've tried all sorts of other things to find good salespeople, including psychometric testing, recruitment companies and everything else I can think of, over a period of 30 years. I've hired dozens. The sad fact is that about 2/3 of the salespeople I've hired have been duds. After 30 years I'm resigned to the fact that if I want to hire *one* new salesperson I actually have to go through the process up to *three* times.

All salespeople can sell well at a job interview, and about a third of them can actually sell your product or service. Perhaps there is some mysterious combination of the person, your service, and the market that either works, or doesn't. The only advice I'd give is to keep them on a short leash: give them a target to meeting during their probation period (usually three months) and fire them *without fail* if they don't meet it. Letting them stay because they've got 'a lot of irons in the fire' will only extend your (and their) agony.

Online and other promotions

One of the tools in your sales toolkit will be online promotion. But despite what you hear, it's unlikely to be the beginning and end of your sales activity, not in the B2B space anyway.

After all, even if your business runs completely online, with you emailing customers you find through social media and then making their purchases through your web site without even making a phone call ... you can still grow your business more by making a few outgoing calls. If you have the kind of business that generates cash while you sit on the beach, get off the beach and go make some *more* sales.

Online promotion is a great way to find potential customers, or for them to find you, but for most businesses it's only the start of the process. After all, every single online sale and every single online enquiry starts with a live, breathing human being. And the web hasn't created any more of them (dating sites aside!), just provided a different way for you to talk to them.

Think of online promotion the same way you think of mass mailing, or radio ads, or PR, or billboards. Just one more way of many many ways to find your customers.

And if your customers are easy to find, then don't waste money on anything more than phone calls. If you sell to government departments, then you know where they are and you can find their phone numbers: in that circumstance why would you waste time on a PR campaign, or on search engine optimisation, when you can just pick up the phone?

When you're trying to find customers, focus on 'target-rich environments', places where your customers are likely to congregate either in person or with their attention. If you sell to Office Managers, is there an Officer Manager Conference coming up? Or is there an Office Management Monthly that you can write an article for? Or do they all hang out in the same bar? The more focussed your promotion, the more response you're going to get.

Sales metrics

It's vitally important for the growth of your business that you know what works and what doesn't. In sales that means tracking where your sales come from, so that you can optimise the amount of money and time that you spend on each activity.

Even large organisations fall into the trap of taking out expensive ads and then not tracking the effect those ads have on sales. Ad agencies will tell you that advertising "increases the value of your brand" without actually being able to tell you how much that is worth in sales.

When you ask an ad agency questions like "how many extra widgets will I sell as a result of this ad", they will look at you with what they hope is a pitying expression. They will patiently explain that only the commercially naive will ever ask a question like that. But they're completely and utterly wrong, at best ignorant and at worst dishonest.

Every sales and promotional activity you undertaken can be measured, and very simply. Just make sure that every lead you get is recorded, along with its source.

That can be as simple as a spreadsheet. The one we use here has the following columns:

- Date
- Source (Google, Referral, Outbound call, etc)

- Details (Google search terms, person who referred, etc)
- Client
- What they wanted
- Quality (1=tyre kicker to 5=excellent)
- Value of the sale (if it's made)

By being careful about collecting this information, and then by going back to analyse it and filling in the sale value, you can measure exactly what return you're getting from every promotional activity you run. The only slight downside is that you have to ask incoming callers where they found you.

Using a simple tool like this you can make informed decisions about whether that Yellow Pages ad paid for itself, or whether your Google ads are worthwhile.

Building your business

The information in this book will give you enough knowledge to start a business, or improve sales for an existing business.

Unfortunately, sales needs more than just knowledge, it needs practice and experience. If you have the chance to work with an experienced salesperson, take it - there are always things that you can learn in the field that you can never get out of books.

And don't be afraid to fail. If you're just starting out, pick a non-critical customer (a small one perhaps) to practice on. Expect to stuff up, and don't beat yourself up over it. Sales takes time to learn, and not all learning is done through success.

If you are just starting a business, I'd also like to recommend the other book in this series "Actually Useful Accounting" (available through Amazon). It will give you a handle on how to avoid cash flow problems, and advice on everything from tax to insurance.

What's next?

If you'd like to see what other books I've written, you can do that here:

```
amazon.com/author/philcohen
```

Much of what I've written has been fiction (but not this book, honest!).

If you're about to start your own company, congratulations. I've been running companies for many decades and I can tell you that it's the most fun you can have sitting down.

www.ingramcontent.com/pod-product-compliance
Lightning Source LLC
Chambersburg PA
CBHW071756170526
45167CB00003B/1049